# MoreLondonPeculiars

## Being curious corners of a capital city

## Peter Ashley

ENGLISH HERITAGE

Published by English Heritage, Isambard House, Kemble Drive, Swindon SN2 2GZ

www.english-heritage.org.uk

English Heritage is the Government's statutory advisor on all aspects of the historic environment.

First published 2007

10 9 8 7 6 5 4 3 2 1

ISBN-10 1 85074 999 X

ISBN-13 978 185074 999 8

Product code 51183

*British Library Cataloguing in Publication Data*

A CIP catalogue for this book is available from the British Library.

Edited and brought to publication by René Rodgers, English Heritage Publishing

Page layout by Michael McMann

Printed in Dubai by Oriental Press

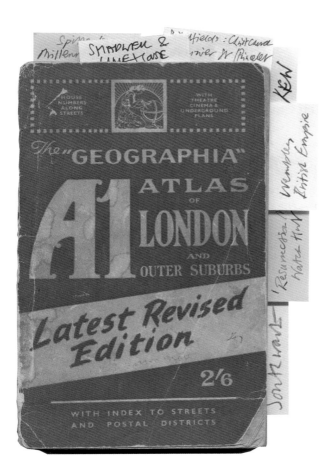

# CONTENTS

# FOREWORD

One can imagine the quiz question: 'What do the Gherkin, the Woolwich Ferry and Queenstown Road Station have in common?' This would surely be the perfect way to silence a pub. The answer, of course, is that they all qualify as London Peculiars, in this, the second volume that records the everyday world which surrounds us in London.

Needless to say, one might have lived in London for years and simply never noticed a Peculiar that has possibly lain only a few feet from where one has walked, sat or visited many times before. We must all have our favourites – whether it be the nude figure on the Fortune Theatre, the cast-iron dolphins that embrace the Embankment street lamps or that most remarkable marble Hindu temple at Neasden. Suddenly, here they all are, gathered in the poignant photographs of Peter Ashley. He sees things that somehow we don't. It makes me feel mole-like, caught up blind in daily concerns about meeting times, train timetables and the eternal interruption of mobile telephone calls. If only one had time to see, then the pleasures of London would unfold, tumbling out of the drab grey stonework like the winnings of some great urban one-armed-bandit.

This book takes one away from the standard sights of London – the things that you should see, the things the historians value and the tourists photograph. This seems to be a book designed for the residents and users of the city. Who but the most unflagging tourist would pay a visit to the Abbey Mills Pumping Station? And yet were they to do so, they would find one of the most sensational Victorian palaces in the world – and all devoted to the joys of sewage treatment. And then there are those extraordinary railings to the council blocks at Oval made out of old wartime stretchers. I have not yet seen these, but will make a point of doing so. In our current age of environmental concern and recycling, this should inspire us to make better use of our waste.

Defining what makes a Peculiar seems quite a challenge. 'Peculiar' by definition means out of the ordinary and yet all of the Peculiars listed in this book can be readily seen in ordinary day-to-day life. I suspect that none of them were created to be self-consciously 'peculiar', they have just become so, partly due to their survival in a changing world, and partly because they were pretty eccentric to begin with. All of the Peculiars appear handmade in some way, quirky, individual and considered, unique to their location. Some Peculiars are so ephemeral, that they may not even survive the time that it will take for this book to be published. The old printing trade union initials on the building on Blackfriars Road, Southwark – at one time surely the bane of newspaper proprietors – are now a mere shadowy sequence of meaningless letters that are largely unrecognised.

The sense of a passage of time is the most enduring feature of this book. It is a snapshot in time and is now already out of date. Peter Ashley's views are recorded for posterity and, unlike so much that is published, the older this book becomes, the more interesting and vital it will be. London as a city seems to be changing faster than ever. While Peter Ashley optimistically ends with the suggestion that new Peculiars are being created all the time, sadly one fears that more of the old Peculiars are lost each year than meaningful new ones made. Magnificent though the new Wembley stadium may be, it could be anywhere in the world and is not unique in the way of those splendid old twin towers – which could and perhaps should have been kept alongside the new. I fear that we will come to lament their passing. One also wonders whether the new Olympic quarter in the east will have the necessary local ingredients that will make it 'London' rather than anywhere else. The riverscape of the Thames is already witness to this internationalist approach, where clusters of slabs of mass-constructed private housing in a medley of Iberian-marine styles now extend from Putney to Greenwich. The result is awful. Soon there will be high-rise block clusters at Vauxhall, Waterloo and Southwark, casting shadows on what is left below. Perhaps these will be the new London Peculiars, although one fears they will become more of the London banalities that we are already subconsciously trying to block out.

For now, Peter Ashley brings the joy of the city to this book and there is still more work for him to do. I once paused in a traffic jam on the Marylebone Road to see a curious and perfectly preserved Art Deco glazed front to a shop that sold dress costume. It still had its stylish metal letters intact and I was instantly taken back to the 'Mr Benn' of my childhood. Can it still be there, I wonder? And then another pause, this time on a train, at a deserted platform at Battersea Park Station. There was a high-backed timber bench on the platform that was being repainted, while the platform beyond was made entirely of old wooden railway sleepers. A bearded figure in a long Victorian coat would not have looked out of place. And finally, that extraordinary urban sequence from the south on the former A102(M) Blackwall Tunnel Approach Road. First one passes an old tenement block built, very unusually, of red sandstone but now surrounded by piles of spoil and chimneys, which looks like the opening scene of a murder film set in Glasgow. A split second beyond, behind hideous concrete overhead gantries and signs, one sees a glimpse of the handsome purple granite portal of the original Blackwall Tunnel, inscribed with proud black letters commemorating its original Victorian construction. The 1960s traffic engineers have done everything in their power to prevent this from being seen, as if embarrassed by something fine that was not of their creation. If Peter Ashley can photograph this – perhaps the most dangerously sited London Peculiar – then he's a braver man than I.

**Ptolemy Dean**

If evidence was needed of how London shifts and adapts, the outlook constantly dissolving like scene changes in a flickering film, one need only think of what has occurred since the publication of the first volume of Peculiars. The 17th-century London gateway, the Temple Bar, has finally returned from rural Hertfordshire, back to within a quick Hansom cab ride of its original site at the top of Fleet Street. Police Public Call Posts have appeared in the City again – pristine, bright blue metal officers standing to attention on the pavement. They are surreally bereft of any communication skills other than to tell you that if you urgently want to talk to a real policeman you must use the nearest payphone, but at least they're back on some kind of virtual beat. Unlike the Routemaster bus – predictably, this much loved London

icon was just too good to stay on the streets, too user-friendly, too much of an original. The end to regular services came when Arriva No. 159 made its last journey on Friday 9 December 2005 from Marble Arch to Brixton. Feelings ran high as the pavements were jammed with those who mourned its passing. I suspect its demise is really about wanting London to look 'cutting edge' for the 2012 Olympic Games, although I would have thought passengers doing back flips off the rear platform of a Routemaster would have been just the ticket. Happily at the time of writing it appears that one or two are still working tourist routes.

Thank goodness some of the things that make London by far the most interesting capital in the world are immutable. I said in my introduction to *London Peculiars* (2004) that I hadn't managed to find the council flat railings made out of Second World War ARP stretchers. They began to take on the illusive cloak of urban myth, but two kind correspondents took pity on me and pointed me in the right direction, so they've made it into this volume. And then Iain Sinclair wrote and told me that if I'd watched Patrick Keiller's film *London* (1994), the mystery of the railings would have been solved. 'He has a nice shot of them, twinned with the now vanishing Routemaster buses.' Hold very tight please. Ding ding.

That's one of the many pleasures of hunting down Peculiars, wherever they might be. Someone will nearly always know the answers, make the connections. (Equally someone will always be willing to make something up.) So when I finally discovered my stretchers one rainy afternoon in Kennington I shouted for joy, much to the consternation of a nearby bus queue.

Other Peculiars are more vulnerable. I was amazed to find the biggest collection of prefabs in the country hiding behind hedges in remote Catford. I wouldn't have known about them if I hadn't discovered Greg Stevenson's classic *Palaces for the People* (2003). Nearly all of them were flying Union flags and had posters in the windows defying the local council who, I would imagine, are itching to let someone build twice as many houses on the land if only they could get the bulldozers in. I worry too about the last surviving remnants of the 1924 British Empire Exhibition on Olympic Way in Wembley. The original Palaces of Arts and Industry are now surrounded, hopefully only temporarily, by blighted hinterlands of decay, the Exhibition's lion's-head motifs blindly roaring at the giant backside of the new Wembley Stadium rising up in front of them.

I have also found equally obsessive allies in my new searches. Architectural dab hand Philip Wilkinson told me about the recently renewed Carreras cigarette factory in Mornington Crescent and warned me not to get overexcited. I did. Ptolemy Dean grabbed me by the Seven Dials in Covent Garden and started poking his finger at a lamp post languishing on one of the street corners, displaying a long-forgotten coat of arms. And my intrepid band of followers on our London walks drew my attention to oddities I would have otherwise missed as I strode on to the next Peculiar port-of-call. Thank you everybody.

But once again most of these new Peculiar discoveries have introduced themselves to me by metaphorically tapping me on the shoulder during my disorganised ramblings about the capital. King Lud and his ghostly companions frightened the life out of me in their dark recess in St Dunstan's; Bates's cat stared glassily at me from between Ecuador coffee planters' hats in Jermyn Street; an unselfconscious nude in easy-to-assemble pieces stared past me in Waterloo; a provocative girl on her controversial plinth ignored splashing tourists at her feet; and a mythical beast crawling down a canopied fountain grimaced in stony horror at overhearing television sound bites on a Westminster Village Green. All counterpoints to the teeming life around them.

These things we need, the fixed points that can mark our London journeys, the map pins of our personal geographies. Whenever I take a train out of Waterloo I always look out for one of my markers at Queenstown Road Station. At the same level as the raised platform is the upper storey of a red brick building in the road below. On the parapet is a sign painted on the brickwork: 'Dining Rooms' in big white capitals on a pale blue ground. The very phrase is so evocative of another time, another age. There is a café underneath but I don't imagine it consists of any 'Dining Rooms' with meat and two veg, hot gravy, steamy bustle and white aprons. Other people, like the Cutting Edges who got shot of the Routemaster, will probably think 'What's that still doing there?' and start ordering brick-coloured paint from Central Stores on their Bluetooths or whatever. Don't let them. We really do need our London Peculiars.

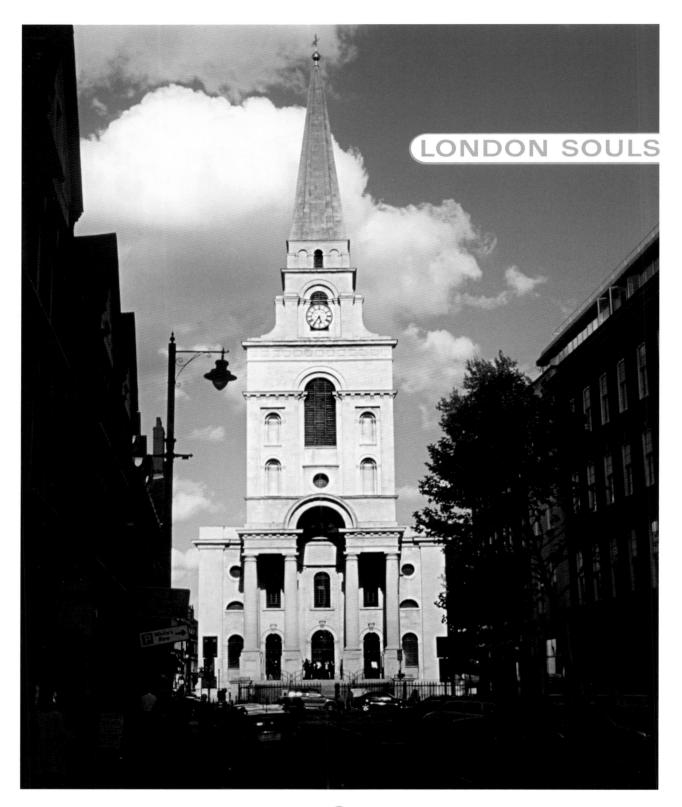

LONDON SOULS

# Hawksmoor Churches

*...in the maddest of Hawksmoor's designs there is always architectural and religious logic.*
Ian Nairn, *Nairn's London*, 1988

You can never ignore a Hawksmoor church. Something about it will always draw you in, activate a 'hang-on-a-minute' moment. Nairn was right – they look like churches and they appear to follow the brief as far as liturgical requirements go, but only just. They get lumped in with the baroque, but in my book they are simply Hawksmoor, amongst the most beautiful, enigmatic and slightly eerie churches in London – white Portland stone codes still waiting to be deciphered. When the wooden scaffolding poles came off, the impact on early 18th-century sensibilities must have been like waking up to see Foster's Gherkin (*see* p 119) on the skyline. Peter Ackroyd got so excited about Hawksmoor's churches after reading Iain Sinclair's poem *Lud Heat* that he wrote a bestseller, *Hawksmoor*, where he juggled an 18th-century architect called Nicholas Dyer with a 20th-century copper called Hawksmoor. It is a truly frightening book, full of dark secrets and sacrificial boys being chucked off scaffolding.

Nicholas Hawksmoor (1661–1736) started his London career as a clerk to Christopher Wren, became his pupil, assistant and finally business partner and then worked for John Vanbrugh. Both these figures tended to overshadow his own achievements – Hawksmoor as 'back room boy'. But he was their friend and they gave him the respect and encouragement that underpinned his own truly independent concepts. Hawksmoor designed many buildings, amongst them the Castle Howard Mausoleum and the twin towers of Westminster Abbey, but here and on pp 12–15 is his classic triumvirate of East End churches and his only City church, all built as a result of the New Churches Act of 1711.

## Christ Church Spitalfields (1714–29)
### ⊖ Liverpool Street

This is probably my favourite Hawksmoor church, a great white rocket poised over the market and the desirable silk weavers' houses to the north. Viewed from way down Brushfield Street (*opposite*) it's almost as if the tower is balanced on stilts in front of another building. As you move closer and cross the road into Fournier Street (*below*), the illusion vanishes and you realise that the stilts are in fact the Tuscan columns of a vast portico. You will also see that the tower isn't the predictable square but an austere rectangular slab and that on the base of one of the columns is engraved an 1843 notice about where to obtain the engine key in case of fire.

The crypt was emptied here to make way for an extended café, which was quite a formidable operation, as you can imagine. They discovered a jumble of collapsed coffins, some containing almost perfectly preserved corpses. How many of these souls, I wonder, listened to sermons here that comforted them with the thought that they would rest in peace until Judgement Day?

## St George-in-the-East, Stepney (1714–19)
**DLR** Shadwell

This is the one Hawksmoor church (*left*) you can really stand back from to see how it all works. On The Highway between Whitechapel and Limehouse, it shines out in dazzling stone, almost economic in its lack of overt decoration with sheer surfaces and recessed window openings that are both angular and round-headed. But it's almost as if Hawksmoor got fed up with his self-imposed restraint and at the last minute pencilled in the four pepper-pot turrets (*below left*) over the gallery staircases. They work superbly, but Mr Nairn couldn't get to grips with them, thinking them sinister: 'This is a stage beyond fantasy, which is always comfortably related to common sense: it is the more-than-real world of the drug addict's dream.'

## St Anne's, Limehouse (1714–30)
**DLR** Westferry

Every time I drive by St Anne's (*right*) I have to stop and just stare at it. At night it's a very spooky place; I half expect to see the shadows of Lascars on the white surfaces, scurrying off to an opium den. There used to be a gloomy pub opposite the east end called the Five Bells and Blade Bone, which didn't help.

But in the early morning sunlight St Anne's looks magnificent with its tower gathering together bell openings, pilasters, columns and obelisks for a sky-piercing finale. Go into Newell Street and see the scale of the west front through the narrow gap in the houses, the view filled with the immense circular vestibule that projects from the tower base. St Anne's reputedly has London's highest church clock and was once the official church for the registration and baptism of babies born at sea. It was certainly used as a landmark by shipping manoeuvring up Limehouse Reach. Imagine looking out over the Thames from Rotherhithe and seeing it rising up over the rooftops and a forest of sailing ship masts and spars.

# St Mary Woolnoth (1717–27) ⊖ Bank

Appearing to be shoehorned into an incredibly tight space between King William Street and Lombard Street is Hawksmoor's only City church – probably the most interesting church in the square mile. St Mary Woolnoth of the Nativity, to give it its full title, was first mentioned in 1191, albeit as 'Wlnotmaricherche'. It was replaced in 1438 and renovated by Wren after damage from the Great Fire in 1666, but this building proved unsafe. After 10 years of rebuilding by Hawksmoor – paid for by a surplus of old sea coal tax – it reopened on Easter Day 1727.

Once again it's the tower (*right*) that grabs the attention, giving here an impression that two separate towers have theatrically merged into one whilst keeping individual turrets at the top. Inside there is a suitably overpowering pulpit (*top left*) – also by Hawksmoor and a useful backdrop for hellfire and brimstone sermons – and black wooden panels around the walls, which you suddenly realise are the fronts off galleries now removed.

Can you believe they actually wanted to pull all this down to make way for Bank Station? Good sense prevailed and the massive cube of stone was shored up at great expense so that work could continue underneath. Evidence of the close proximity of the tube can be seen in the tiny front churchyard behind the railings in King William Street (*bottom left*), where an original entrance to the station can still be seen – admirably fitting in like a doorway into a crypt – which, in fact, is exactly where the original City & South London Railway ticket office was.

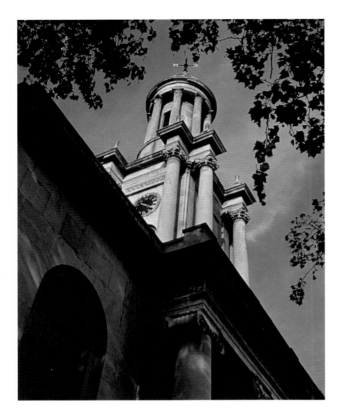

## Holy Trinity, Marylebone Road
### ⊖ Great Portland Street

Sir John Soane built this church (1824–8) to serve the expanding population in the area. It was the most expensive of three churches he designed for the Church Commissioners, part of a spate of building that became known as 'Waterloo' churches, built in celebration of the victory that finally brought the protracted Napoleonic wars to an end. The Duke of Wellington was in fact a parishioner, along with J M W Turner and William Gladstone. Florence Nightingale was also a regular member of the congregation.

The architecture is better explained elsewhere, but two interesting aspects emerge when one starts to dig a little deeper. The first is the curiosity of an outside pulpit on the south entrance front, a strange orientation in itself that puts the altar to the north. It was put here to commemorate the life of Canon William Cadman whose preaching drew large crowds for the 50 years of his ministry. And what a fitting memorial – the plaque says it all in the chosen text from Hebrews: 'He being dead yet speaketh.'

Holy Trinity is also a landmark in the search for new uses for redundant churches. For many years this was an SPCK bookshop and offices, and another bookish connection came during the Second World War. Penguin Books had moved into offices above a car showroom in Great Portland Street opposite the church and part of the crypt (that had served as an air-raid shelter in the First World War) was used for storing their increasingly popular paperbacks. On occasion those working down below the church forgot about services taking place above and the solemnity of worship was interrupted by sepulchral and inappropriate language rising up into the nave.

## St John's, Smith Square ⊖ Westminster

In the Bedfordshire countryside at Wrest Park is a stunning garden building by Thomas Archer, built in 1709–11 (*bottom right*). When I first saw it I didn't know much about Archer, only that his pavilion suddenly made a meteoric entry into my architectural Hit Parade. If he could do this in a garden, what could he do in a London square?

I found out one exceptionally hot morning when I walked into Smith Square. All that could be seen at first was this white tower up in the trees (*top right*), so brilliant it reduced everything else around it to the deepest blues. Closer inspection revealed three more towers, one at each corner of what Pevsner describes as 'the boldest manifestation of English Baroque in Inner London'. Archer's church of St John's (1714–28) is dreamlike, slightly unreal and mysterious, akin to the imaginings of his contemporary Hawksmoor. In 1826 an exact copy of one of the towers was used for Normanton church, now marooned out on Rutland Water.

Charles Dickens didn't like it much. In *Our Mutual Friend* he thought it 'a very hideous church … resembling some petrified monster, frightful and gigantic, on its back with its legs in the air'. It took everyone by surprise when it was built, giving vent to an unlikely story where Archer asks Queen Anne what sort of church she'd like and she kicks over her footstool and says 'like that'. Raising the question of whether this is also the reason why the Dome looks like an overturned barbeque.

St John's was gutted by fire in 1742 and bombed in the war, but it was then that the superb acoustics were recognised and the church was converted into a first-rate concert hall. There's a restaurant in the old crypt called, of course, The Footstool.

## Neasden Temple ⊖ Stonebridge Park, Neasden

The oddest thing about this incredible temple is that it should be in Neasden of all places. The eye wants to put it out on a parched sun-bleached plain or at least towering over ochre-coloured buildings with vultures wheeling around the pinnacles. Of course there is no earthly reason why it shouldn't be in Neasden, it's just that anybody who reads *Private Eye* will know this suburb as an essential part of the satirical magazine's London mythology, the home of Neasden FC and Sid and Doris Bonkers. Willy Rushton sang a song about it, very loudly: 'Neasden, where the birds sing in the treesden...'

I think the Shri Swaminarayan Mandir will alter perceptions forever. This is the largest stone Hindu Mandir in the western

hemisphere. The figures are mind-boggling: 2,820 tons of Bulgarian limestone and 2,000 tons of Italian Carrara marble were shipped to India. Here over 1,500 craftspeople carved 26,300 jigsaw pieces that were then brought to London and reassembled on the corner of Brentfield Road and Meadow Garth. The features' statistics are worth listing just for the names: 7 Shikhars (Pinnacles), 6 Ghummats (Domes), 193 Sthambhas (Pillars), 32 Gavakshas (Windows) and 4 Zarukhas (Balconies). And 2 marble fire escapes. It was opened in 1995 and in its first 10 years over 3 million people found their way here to see a truly incongruous but wondrous sight rising up over the brick terraces of a north London suburb.

## St Mary at Hill ⊖ Monument

Hidden away between Lovat Lane and St Mary at Hill, this Wren church – which gives the street its name – remarkably survived Victorian 'improvement', demolition to facilitate a railway extension and the Blitz, only to suffer a disastrous fire in 1988 and an IRA bomb in 1992. The interior, now restored, is a beautiful space with a rebuilt organ that replicates the original, which was peculiar in having the black and white keys reversed.

Outside, the prodigious wall clock is of a form familiar in the City, where rods attached to mechanisms in the towers operated the hands. Except that here the tower is in Lovat Lane. So although now run by electricity, the clock was once driven remotely by rods that made a considerable journey of 100 feet through the upper spaces of the church interior. Apparently you could stand in the street and watch the minute hand jump every four minutes, should you be so inclined.

The churchyard was once much bigger until a large portion was sold off to accommodate Victorian offices. This was a famous haunt of rooks and when their perches were reduced to just two trees by his new building, Sir Henry Peek ensured that places for them were built into the brickwork. Peter Jackson, in his inimitable *London is Stranger than Fiction* (1951), depicts them as nesting boxes; these circular recesses do seem somewhat narrow for rooks, but the idea is surely clinging on here somewhere.

## St Bartholomew the Great ⊖ Barbican

Just off West Smithfield a half-timbered gateway (*top right*) sits between the shops and wine bars. This is an amazing survivor – although extensively restored this is the original 13th-century entrance into the nave of an Augustinian priory. The footpath leading down to the church was once part of this nave and the original south aisle wall can still be seen on the right.

When we go into a Wren or a Hawksmoor London church we have a certain positive fix on the era we're dealing with. These are the works of architects and named craftsmen and although 300 or so years have passed we still manage to make the connections. But come into St Bartholomew the Great and the imagination has to work overtime to sift through the shadows. This is Henry I's thanksgiving for getting over malaria – a world of dodgy prelates, chain-mailed knights, pedlars and awestruck peasantry, all somehow made stone in these fat Norman columns.

Then suddenly there's an odd hint of domesticity up on the south side of the chancel: an oriel window (*bottom right*) that should be looking out over box parterres and pleached trees bearing medlars and quinces. It once served an early 16th-century private oratory where Prior William Bolton could worship near to his lodgings but still keep an eye on things below. In later times Bolton would not have been best pleased to look out and see beneath him a blacksmith's forge, a hop store and stables in the cloisters. But after Sir Aston Webb's very sympathetic restorations, begun in 1884, the Norman past was once again revealed in all its uncompromising glory.

## Bunhill Fields ⊖ Old Street, Moorgate

There aren't many places in London that I would recommend you visit in the rain, but Bunhill Fields is a particular pleasure on a wet late spring or summer afternoon. Perhaps it's something to do with the all-enveloping dome of leaves filtering light down over the graves and tomb chests, the steady pattering of raindrops gathering and dripping as if from the edge of a green umbrella. You won't find a church, for Bunhill Fields is no churchyard. This is a last resting place for Nonconformists, a City survivor of numerous small burial grounds consecrated for Dissenters.

It's reckoned that upwards of 120,000 bodies were buried here on the 4 acres of land that stretch between Moorgate and Bunhill Row, evidence of the cheek-by-jowl nature of London burials before the industrial-scale Victorian cemeteries were laid out on the fringes of the capital. The graves include three famous names – William Blake, John Bunyan and Daniel Defoe; visionaries and dreamers resting where magpies chatter their orations up in the bright green canopy. The paths that cut through the burial ground are separated from the graves by iron railings and there's a very useful map at the central crossing point.

## St Olave's Gateway, Seething Lane
⊖ Tower Hill

Charles Dickens loved the peculiar in London. One of his favourite spots was the little churchyard between Hart Street and Seething Lane, with its trio of skulls in the curved pediment of the entrance. In *The Uncommercial Traveller* he writes: 'Such strange churchyards hide in the City of London' and noted that St Olave's was 'one of my best beloved churchyards which I call the churchyard of Saint Ghastly Grim … It is a small, small churchyard with a ferocious spiked iron gate like a jail. This gate is ornamented with skulls and crossbones larger than life, wrought in stone; [and] thrust through and through with iron spears.' A very welcoming sight.

There is talk of a burial pit here for victims of the Great Plague of 1665 and this would certainly explain the ghastly grimness of the gateway decoration, but 17th-century England was often preoccupied with skulls and bones as the ultimate metaphors for death. The church itself survived the Great Fire in 1666 only to be severely damaged in the Blitz, but it was restored in 1954 and with a garden having now replaced the churchyard, it remains an unspoilt corner of the City. The bodies of Samuel Pepys and his wife Elizabeth are buried beside the Communion table.

## Giro's grave, Carlton House Terrace
### ⊖ Piccadilly Circus

Poke your nose through the railings at the top of the Duke of York's Steps and you will see this wood-and-glass box. It protects the tombstone of a dog named Giro with an inscription in German: 'Giro: ein treuer Begleiter!' or 'Giro: a true companion!' It also has a date, February 1934, and the name Hoesch.

Dr Leopold von Hoesch was the German ambassador from 1932–6 and the stone commemorates his pet Alsatian. This was originally the garden to 9 Carlton House Terrace, which was the German Embassy at the time. Hoesch was the last ambassador from the Weimar Republic, which preceded the Nazis' rise to power, and, dying in office, he was granted a full diplomatic funeral that entailed a 19-gun salute in Hyde Park. Apparently there is a photograph in the archives of The Royal Society – current occupiers of No. 9 – that bizarrely shows Grenadier Guards bearing Hoesch's coffin whilst the Embassy staff jostle each other on the steps in order to give the Nazi salute. Such was life's rich pageant in the London of 1936 as Hitler installed Joachim von Ribbentrop as Hoesch's successor.

## Watcher's hut, Wanstead ⊖ Wanstead

Wanstead can be easily missed as you arrive
in London on the M11 and negotiate the
Redbridge roundabout. To either side of
Eastern Avenue are quiet suburban streets,
in and out of which are reminders of 18th-
century development that took advantage of
the proximity of the popular coaching route to
and from Colchester. To the south are
Overton Drive and the church of St Mary, built
in 1787–90 by Thomas Hardwick in precisely

jointed ashlar. Walk round to the south side and a large leafy churchyard opens up filled with interesting tombs under the trees. And hidden amongst the shrubberies is a curious tapering stone sentry box, built in memory of the Wilton family in 1831.

This is a watcher's hut, where a sentry would indeed have guarded the churchyard. This was a time of body snatchers, when fresh corpses for medical research were hard to come by unless removed from their graves at the earliest opportunity, naturally under the cover of darkness. A watchman was paid to sit in here and look out for the light from a swaying lantern and to listen for the first sharp incision of a spade into mouldering soil. But what an elegant solution for what is after all just an open-sided hut. Imagine what we would have to put up with here today if an invasion of the body snatchers became popular again. I suppose the best a night watchman could hope for would be something pressed out of durable plastic like a Portaloo.

Evidence of London's past lives on far beyond its time and some of the most intriguing can be found in the traces of lettering that still give out signals like a forgotten spaceship on a remote planet. They could be as durable as terracotta or gilded glass, vulnerable as paint on a wall or a wooden gate, but many signs have also benefited from the efforts of enlightened individuals who have been their jealous guardians or even their appreciative restorers.

## Highbury Station ⊖ Highbury & Islington

Opposite the Underground station on the north side of Holloway Road is the original station entrance, built in 1904 for the Great Northern & City Railway and called just 'Highbury'. Disused since April 1968 the five glazed arches languished for some time behind poster hoardings, but now not only are these removed to reveal the frontage but someone has also taken care to highlight the original lettering.

## Middlesex Artists' Rifles, Dukes Road
### ⊖ Euston

In the mid-1970s I walked by this building every day and never gave it a second glance, probably because it was a dance school called The Place and the girls sitting outside proved an agreeable distraction. Until recently, that is, when I happened to go by on the other side of the road and saw this terracotta plaque and the lettering 'Middlesex Artists' Rifles'. This was the regimental drill hall designed by their colonel, R W Edis, in 1888–9 and the badge depicts Mars and Minerva, sculpted by Thomas Brock.

The Artists' Rifles was formed in 1860 by Edward Sterling and amongst those who came to attention in their Victorian ranks were William Holman Hunt, John Everett Millais and William Morris. But it's the names of some of the volunteers in the First World War that have probably reached out to us most over the intervening years: poets Wilfred Owen and Edward Thomas and painter Paul Nash, a survivor of the horror.

**Crispin Street, Spitalfields**
⊖ **Liverpool Street**

I have photographed Donovan Bros twice, once in the late 1980s when I got up extremely early to go and see Spitalfields Market at work. As I snapped away at traders loading up vans with fruit and veg, one of them very obligingly put an apple crate over his head for me. This was when Donovan's was painted red and gloriously scruffy like everything else. The market has all but gone now, replaced by City boys and girls washed up from Bishopsgate, drinking Americanos and staring at their Blackberries. Donovan's has emigrated to Essex, but they still produce essential paper goods for the market trade. Their old offices are now dark green, but thankfully the fabulously characterful lettering survives.

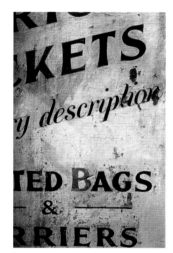

## Queenstown Road Station ⇌

This little station is two stops out of Waterloo. It's where they bring new railway recruits to teach them how dangerous it is to run across the tracks. But it also appears to be the station that time forgot. Up on the island platform you can see across to a disused platform that is slowly sinking into the ground with a useful notice saying 'Do Not Alight Here', but it's down below where it gets really interesting.

I can't offer any explanation for the booking hall (*below*), which seems to be in a time warp. It appears as it did 60 years ago, tricked out in the wonderfully evocative Southern Railway style of the time. At first I thought it must be for a film until I studied the plate above the notice board and saw that it seemed to be genuine. Maybe I'd slipped back to 1946 and if I'd looked more carefully perhaps I was also in a tweed suit with a trilby and brown brogues and a copy of the *News Chronicle* under my arm. Check the CCTV footage.

It carries on outside (*above right*), taking us even further back in time. The station fascia is still proclaiming ownership by the London & South Western Railway, which operated under that name from 1839 to 1923, and the station name is 'Queen's Road'. Only Gerry Barney's brilliant 1960s British Rail symbol, now a generic for all stations, puts us firmly in our own time. But this still seems to be a station for ghost trains to shuffle into at ungodly hours.

## Dundee Courier, Fleet Street
### ⊖ Temple, Blackfriars

Newspaper offices once filled Fleet Street and its environs, the smoky pubs and wine bars awash with journalists swapping copy and gossip over copious drinks. Lorries backed up to unloading bays with giant rolls of newsprint and everywhere was the sound of the latest inky headlines being printed or being thumped onto the floors of those urgent vans with big stripes all over them. Come the revolution everyone disappeared off into Docklands and the 'Street of Shame', as *Private Eye* has it, fell silent.

But the memories live on. Here a nondescript brick building next to St Dunstan's church is wonderfully enlivened by mosaic panels listing newspaper and magazine titles. This was the London outpost of Dundee publishers D C Thomson who still publish most of these titles in one form or another. But the really important names from their stable are missing. Where are those comic essentials *The Beano* and *The Dandy*?

## Daily Express, Fleet Street ⊖ Blackfriars

Further down Fleet Street is the stunning Daily Express building, a jazz hymn to Art Deco in black glass and chrome. The Express name has been built into the fabric of the building with metal cut-out letters. The paper isn't found here anymore, which is sad. These Fleet Street buildings were once reflections of the titles in their halcyon days – the flashy *Daily Express* taking risks, the *Daily Telegraph* next door all staid fluted columns and a clock always telling the correct time, and the *News Chronicle* stuck down a side street.

## Blackfriars Road
⊖ Southwark

This boarded-up building (*right*) still speaks of a piece of trade union history. The worn lettering states that these were the offices, or a local branch, of the National Society of Operative Printers and Assistants. It took me a while to realise that this was of course NATSOPA, scourge of newspaper proprietors and upholders of the lengthy tea break. They merged with the equally impressive National Union of Printing, Bookbinding and Paper Workers (who couldn't wangle an acronym) to form another set of initials: SOGAT, or the Society of Graphical and Allied Trades.

## Abchurch Yard
⊖ Cannon Street

There will often be earlier manifestations of street names in the vicinity of the latest version. Here in the yard in front of Wren's homely brick St Mary Abchurch the fading letters of at least two previous signs can be seen (*left*).

## Commercial Street
## ⊖ Liverpool Street, Shoreditch

Godfrey Phillips started trading as a cigar merchant on this site in 1865, but 50 years later Commercial Street and the little back lanes of Jerome Street, Corbet Place and Hanbury Street saw a slimline Art Deco tobacco factory appear. The name will be familiar to those of a certain age as the company that gave us brands like Ariston Plain and The Greys, which sported a regimental coat of arms, and cigarette cards like 'Famous Cricketers' and 'British Orders of Chivalry and Valour'. But not anymore. The name coughs on in India, but this gilded sign up on a wall in Spitalfields is all that remains in London.

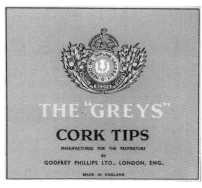

## Hope (Sufferance) Wharf ⊖ Rotherhithe

I have always been intrigued by this lettering on a wall in St Marychurch Street in Rotherhithe. Recently repainted – a promising sign – the lettering not only reminds us of the existence of Hope Wharf but also of the curious adjunct 'sufferance' that once appeared in many wharf names along the Thames. During the 18th century shipping traffic had grown to such an extent that the 'legal' wharves sanctioned to ship and unload cargoes were totally inadequate for the amount of trade. So other wharves, particularly on the south bank, took in business under what was known as 'a sufferance' – that is, 'by tacit consent but without express permission'.

There are many other signs fading away in Docklands and I include two others photographed many years ago. The exact locations have now escaped me, although I do know that Lovell's Wharf was in Greenwich and specialised in scrap iron and that L Noel & Sons were importers of capers, Parmesan cheese, curry powder, anchovies and leaf gelatine from the Mediterranean. They are still an important part of McCormick Herbs and Spices.

## Long Acre ⬌ Covent Garden

The legend reading down into the shadows on Long Acre is 'Armstrong Siddeley' and 'Connaught Coachworks'. In post-war Britain Armstrong Siddeley Sapphires were very elegant six-cylinder motor cars made in Coventry. They started out as Siddeleys, then Siddeley-Deaseys (known, of course, as Diddeley Easeys), finally gaining the prefix Armstrong on amalgamation with the Armstrong Whitworth company. I always thought there was something faintly exotic about them with their Sphinx mascot lying on the bonnet. This lettering still marks the original site of a showroom and workshops.

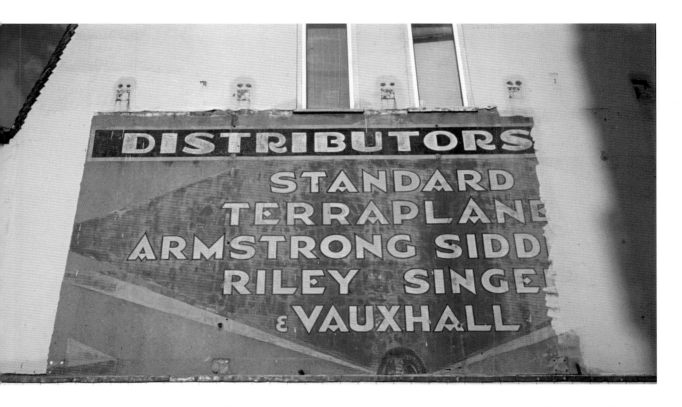

### Heath Road, Twickenham ⇌ Twickenham

The Armstrong Siddeley name also suddenly appeared alongside other famous marques when a poster hoarding was taken down in Twickenham. This wall lettering, on the corner of Tennyson Avenue, is truly remarkable since, one assumes, that it has survived under exhortations to buy baked beans and washing powder since before the Second World War. The clue to dating it comes from 'Terraplane', a product of the American Hudson Motor Company that last produced a car under this stand-alone name in 1937. Hurry before the hoarding goes back or the wall receives a further obliterating coat of paint – this may only be a brief outing into the sunlight. But at least we'll know what's behind the fatuous posters for mobile phones or, even better, the next identikit automobiles.

## Bates, Jermyn Street ⊖ Piccadilly Circus

If more people wore the kind of hats you find in Bates, more people would come in here and buy them rather than just asking to see the stuffed cat. Trouble is, there's not a huge demand for Ecuador Coffee Planters, Fischer Fedoras or even Henley Boaters come to that. But just seeing them stacked up in the window is a peculiar treat and going in to try them on means that you'll see Binks in his glass case. Now well and truly stuffed, Binks walked into the shop as a kitten in 1921 and went to Pussycat Heaven in 1926. Not long for a cat really, but still long enough for him to be loved and admired enough to be given a top hat and a decent cigar to eternally smoke. Surrounded by tweed caps and beautifully labelled Bates's hat boxes, he has a notice tacked to his case that admonishes those in the shop who are only there just to stare back at him.

## Greater London House, Hampstead Road
## ⊖ Mornington Crescent

I first knew this stunning Art Deco building as the home of the advertising agency Young and Rubicam, creators of the slogan 'Beanz Meanz Heinz'. But they weren't the first here – this was once the Black Cat cigarette factory, properly Carreras, whose name has avoided the attentions of the Tobacco Police and been preserved on the entablature.

This was originally the Arcadia Works, built here by Carreras in 1928. At the time it was both the world's largest cigarette factory and largest reinforced-concrete building. Carreras were so proud of it they put it on the back of their cigarette cards (*right*). The company adopted the cat as its symbol, doubtless influenced by the Egyptian cat-headed goddess Bubastis discovered with Tutankhamen's tomb eight

years earlier. With the rise of the Third Reich it was rumoured that Hitler fancied using the building as his UK headquarters should his invasion plans succeed, just as he apparently earmarked the Grand Hotel in Scarborough for when he needed a break from invading other people's countries.

The architects were M E and O H Collins with A G Porri, but the Art Deco ornament was removed in the 1960s, the original bronze cats being put out to Carreras factories in Basildon and Jamaica. Now it's all back, restored in 1999. Imperious tall Egyptian cats flank the doorways and biblical reeds shoot up the columns. Best of all are the cats' heads in their recessed mounts, the black cats of the cigarette pack logo now fully equipped with wire whiskers. Do they twitch with pleasure if someone lights up as they come out of Mornington Crescent Station opposite?

"GRAN-POP," A SERIES OF 50 BY LAWSON WOOD. No 10

ARCADIA WORKS
Hampstead Rd.
London, N.W.

Nine acres of Sunny Idealism; where happy, healthy workpeople make **good** Cigarettes with care, pride and conscience, under the most hygienic manufacturing conditions known in the Tobacco Industry.

CARRERAS Ltd., ARCADIA WORKS, LONDON, ENGLAND.

## Philpot Lane mice ⊖ Monument

This Italianate building on Eastcheap is a colourful riot of architectural detail. Blue barley twist columns frame pink round-headed windows and pigs' and dogs' heads hide up in the eaves. Round the corner in Philpot Lane two brown mice fight over what appears to be a large lump of cheese. What can it mean?

The most likely story is that as the building progressed the workmen became mystified at the disappearance of their packed lunches, only to discover that resourceful mice were responsible. They carved the mice and cheese in an obscure corner to commemorate the sharing of their lunch. A more colourful version, suiting the building better perhaps, is that two workmen argued over the disappearance of their sandwiches, one thinking that the other had stolen his food. A fight ensued on the scaffolding and they fell to their deaths. The mice were carved by their fellows as a memorial. This version substitutes sandwiches for the cheese, but this looks like a good lump of Cheddar to me.

## Lloyds Bank, Strand ⊖ Temple

Whilst photographing the Royal Courts of Justice on the Strand, I inadvertently stepped backwards and found a slimy flying fish staring at me as it flapped its way down a tiled wall. I was in the vestibule of the Law Courts branch of Lloyds Bank and looking round I was confronted by a highly polished display of Doultonware decorative tiles and mosaics. Designed and painted by J H McLennan, the majolica subjects include grotesque fish, lions' heads, acanthus leaves and curious half-naked men flexing their muscles. It's a mix of baroque and Islamic styles, conceived in 1883 not for Lloyds but for the original business here, the Palsgrove Hotel. McLennan was a star at Doulton's – he was still in his teens when he arrived at the Lambeth Studios in 1877 and only a year later he was winning a silver medal at an Alexandra Palace exhibition. He went on to design and paint panels for the Czar of Russia and the King of Siam, and if you go into the bank to change a fiver you'll see more of his work in tiled panels showing scenes from Ben Jonson plays.

## Leopard's heads, Gresham Street
⊖ St Paul's

On the corner of Gresham Street and Aldersgate Street is another of London's little green oases, a shady spot for eating lunch on a hot summer's day. This was the site of the church of St John Zachary, destroyed in the Great Fire of 1666 and now turned into a garden with these fabulous depictions of particularly fierce leopards adorning the wrought-iron gates. The clue to their residence here is to be found opposite in the hallowed halls of the Worshipful Company of Goldsmiths.

The Company is one of the 12 great livery companies in the City of London and has been responsible for hallmarking since 1300 when gold and silver were first marked with a leopard's head by the wardens of the craft. The leopard is still the hallmark of the London Assay Office and appears on the Goldsmiths' coat of arms – 'Quarterly Gules and Azure in first and fourth quarters a Leopard's Head affrontée', as they say. The Company of Goldsmiths restored the little garden and marked their efforts with these particularly fine beasts adorned with villainous whiskers and garden flowers, which were crafted by Paul Allen.

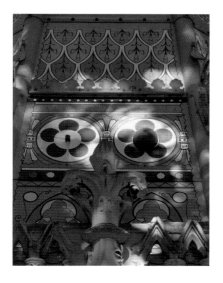

## Buxton Memorial Fountain, Victoria Tower Gardens
⊖ Westminster

They stand out here in all weathers, out in the sun, under umbrellas, muffled against fogs and winter blasts. This is one of Westminster's Village Greens where parliamentarians and television journalists conjoin in their co-dependency to spin and weave the news. They come to these particular spots because MPs always need to give the impression they've just rushed out of Parliament to speak to the nation.

The Victoria Tower will often be the pantomime backdrop, the big flag fluttering proudly in the breeze coming in off the river. But every now and then they get bored and turn the camera round and we'll see this glorious confection in the south of the gardens instead. It looks like an ornate cupola that never made it onto a rooftop, so it comes as no surprise to find that the Buxton Memorial Fountain is a creation of S S Teulon, an English architect who was an aficionado of overpowering Gothic motifs. I'd love to think that this little house, with its pop-eyed leafy lizards and polychrome enamelled roof, was once destined to sit on top of a Gothic fantasia country house in Norfolk.

This wonderfully decorated fountain commemorates the emancipation of slaves in the British Empire in 1834 and was commissioned by Charles Buxton MP. It is another example of a mobile London building, having originally startled passers-by in Parliament Square before arriving here in 1940. There were originally eight figures of British rulers attached to it, all stolen as were their fibreglass replacements.

Where the gardens narrow down to Lambeth Bridge another curious pair of animals flank a white stone seat. Very Pharaonic sheep (*above right*) look distinctly downcast; odd really, as this southernmost corner of the gardens was erected especially for children by the improbably named Harry Gage Spicers in 1923. Behind the sheep's head can be seen the Edwardian Thames House with an early ICI monogram underneath a scallop shell.

## Catford prefabs
### ⇌ Bellingham

As the threat of invasion diminished in the mid-1940s, it was recognised that Britain would need 3–4 million new homes over the next 10 years. Post-war London in particular saw an unprecedented demand for new homes, not only to replace blitzed housing but also to accommodate the postponed marriages and the ensuing baby boom. Traditional building methods simply couldn't cope, so the idea of prefabrication took on a new and urgent relevance. Homes could quite literally be manufactured on a production line, transported on trucks and trailers, and erected on site speedily and cheaply. They were only ever meant to be temporary, but these bright, clean, easily maintained houses were very quickly taken into the hearts of their occupants.

Sixty years on they have all but vanished, cleared away simply because two vastly more expensive houses can be built on a single prefab plot. By 1991 only 300 remained out of a stock of 10,000 in Greater London. And 150 of them are here in Catford, all of them of the Uni-Seco design that cost £1,131 each in 1947. Well-loved and cared for, they are still immediately evocative of the 'Britain Can Make It' mindset of the post-war years. You can still imagine arriving back here from the Festival of Britain in 1951, walking up from Bellingham Station and settling down in your Utility armchair with a mug of Rowntrees cocoa and the *Radio Times* to see what time to tune into Arthur Askey on your Pye wireless set, wondering when rationing will end and whether you have the four coupons necessary to buy a new pair of underpants.

## Spitalfields
### 🚇 Liverpool Street

Huguenot silk weavers came to Spitalfields in the late 17th century and, within a few years, the district was marked out with their 'tenter grounds'. In these areas their woven cloth was washed and stretched on frames called 'tenters', from whence we have the expression 'on tenterhooks'. Early in the 18th century two Somerset-born lawyers, Charles Wood and Simon Michell, bought a tenter ground and a market garden to the north of Nicholas Hawksmoor's Christ Church (see pp 10–11) for development. Silk weavers did take over some of the properties in the area, ultimately converting the upper storeys of these buildings for their trade, but most of the plots were originally taken up by carpenters. Fournier Street, Wilkes Street and Princelet Street were amongst the

most prestigious houses in the neighbourhood, but in the 19th century the area declined and many of the houses had their ground floors given over to shops. But they were, and still are, unique to the character of Spitalfields and, indeed, London.

The Princelet Street photographs (*opposite top and bottom*) show a house with fading and peeling plasterwork and weather-beaten shutters that exemplifies how the streets had decayed. Its companion picture (*above*) shows how Fournier Street is looking now, with something of 17th-century Amsterdam about it. It's all a far cry from 20 years ago when you could walk down the pavement and look through letterboxes at big empty and dusty hallways with staircases ascending into the gloom of upper floors. But something of the spirit of the place still lives on in this celebratory window (*left*).

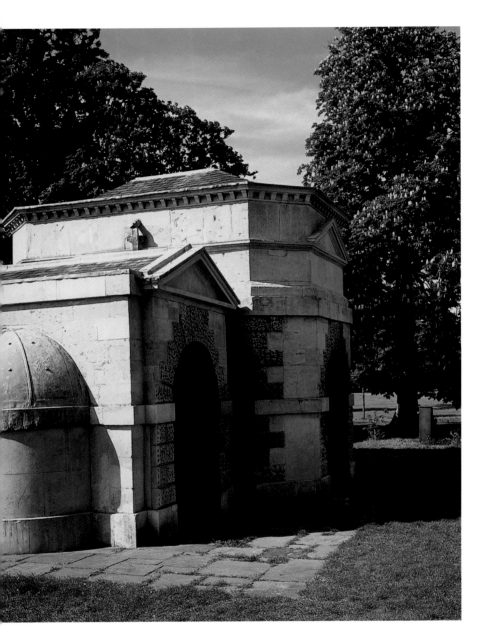

## Queen's Temple, Kensington Gardens
⊖ Lancaster Gate

In 1731 the River Westbourne, now virtually underground for all its length, was turned into the Serpentine by damming a series of pools between Hyde Park and what were originally the grounds to Kensington House. Landscaping in the 18th century also involved designing pavilions and eyecatchers to emphasise viewpoints and to provide recreational shelters. William Kent supplied them here whilst working over at Chiswick for Lord Burlington and only one of these survives: the Queen's Temple. It became a (somewhat cramped) park keeper's house but was restored to its 18th-century form in 1976. You will find it to the south of the Peter Pan statue and east of George Frederick Watt's powerful statue, *Physical Energy*.

## Hanover Gate, Regent's Park ⊖ St Johns Wood, Baker Street

Regent's Park has some of London's most ostentatious buildings on its perimeter. Gwyn Headley, in his text for Lord Snowdon's *London: Sight Unseen* (1999), speculates that the speed at which John Nash was able to develop the park may have had something to do with the relationship between the Prince Regent and the architect's attractive wife Mary Anne. But if all these hasty Nash terraces and crescents get a bit too much, or you're on your way into town after a day's cricket at Lord's, take a look at something smaller like this perfect lodge at the western entrance on Park Road.

I actually prefer it to all the hysteria it announces. The dark trees obscure what is to come, also acting as the perfect backdrop to the square cream stucco building with its chamfered corners, swirling volutes and central chimney stack. Traffic streams around it, oblivious to all its subtle pleasures.

## Millennium Mills, North Woolwich
**DLR Prince Regent**

This is just about the last place in Docklands that still looks like the first reel of the gangster film *The Long Good Friday*. Almost everything else has either vanished or been turned into bleak realisations of glossy ads from the property pages. Spillers' Millennium Mills is a survivor, an uncompromising hulk on the south side of the Royal Victoria Dock.

In the beginning this was a new mill for Vernon & Sons who had 'the world's harvests at their command'. That's a lot of grain, but Vernon's had made their mark in the previous century, winning bread bins full of gold medals for their flour until the Big One – the Miller Cup – was awarded to them on the eve of the millennium in 1899. The grain elevators, silos and mills that subsequently rose over the oily waters became the Millennium Mills, later taken over by Spillers whose name survives in flaking and fading red letters on the parapets.

The mill stands now like an old bruised boxer who's never had to take the final humiliating knockout – battered maybe but not bowed. With soulless apartment blocks, jargon-stuffed conference centres and bark chipping-lined roads leading to nowhere, it's difficult to imagine life here even 40 years ago: the constant low moan of ships' hooters, the safety valve shriek of steam winches and the grinding of gears as Fodens and Albions made for the arterial roads, loaded down with fat, white cotton flour sacks.

There's a slight frisson of fear as one reads the Mayor of London's Planning Decisions for Newham with its mention of '…redevelopment of the site for mixed-use purposes…', but at least it appears that the Millennium Mills will still dominate North Woolwich. I just hope that as they stick in all the ceramic hobs and wireless internet connections someone will think to refurbish the lettering. The original purpose of buildings should never be unthinkingly disguised or forgotten.

## Bryant & May factory,
## Fairfield Road ⊖ Bow Road

Bryant & May stopped making matches in their red brick castle in Bow in 1979, having put little lumps of phosphor on the ends of slivers of wood here since 1861. Now it's called Bow Quarter and it was one of the first manifestations in London of Manhattan-style loft living. It means they've added a kind of penthouse upper story to the main building block that is incongruous, like putting garden sheds on top of the Queen Mary. But the factory still speaks for itself, with its skyline of Italianate towers that supported the sprinkler-system water tanks and cottages that break up the secure walling, features which were once so necessary for such an inflammable industry capable of producing 10,000 million matches a year. I suppose the wall is still useful for keeping the plasma screen

televisions in and riff-raff photographers out.

In 1888 social firebrand Annie Besant lit the blue touchpaper with a magazine article highlighting the dangers of phosphorous fumes at the factory and the low wages of the girls breathing them in. The ensuing strike lasted for three weeks and resulted in landmark concessions and the establishment of a Match Girls Union. An appropriate, if unwitting, symbol of a flaming torch is realised in a pink terracotta panel on one of the cottages with the Latin inscription 'Luce Ex Lucellum'.

### Royal Albert Hall chimney, Kensington Gore
### ⊖ South Kensington (Science Museum exit)

Come here for the Proms, Cream concerts, poetry readings or poppy-strewn remembrances – this is London's village hall. Opened in May 1871 the immense amphitheatre was originally conceived as part of 'Albertopolis', a collection of museums and institutions built on 70 acres of nursery land to the south of Kensington Gardens. Prince Albert started to plan the complex when the 1851 Great Exhibition, which would fund the

project, was just a few weeks away from closing. He died 10 years before the Hall's opening but he is inextricably linked to the building, not only by his imagination but also by his sumptuous memorial that can be found nearby.

The Royal Albert Hall looks circular, but it's actually a red brick oval with a cream terracotta mosaic frieze depicting the Triumph of Arts and Letters and a glass dome. Inside there are three tiers of boxes plus a balcony and gallery where occasional picture exhibitions were displayed. The roof above this gallery held water tanks filled from artesian wells at the Royal Horticultural Society, primed to release their contents in case of fire. Estimates vary as to how many people the Hall holds, but 8,000 seems the safest bet. Circumnavigating the dimly lit corridors at the back of the boxes it could still easily be the 1900s, particularly if there's a choir singing *The Chorus of the Hebrew Slaves*.

Walk up the long flight of steps from Prince Consort Road and at the top turn left. Here you will find this chimney (*right*), isolated on the pavement and once a vital part of the building's operation. The Hall obviously needed to be heated and this is the boiler-house flue, positioned out of the sightlines of most aspects of the building, above the furnaces that were themselves offset from the central area of the Hall.

But the boilers didn't only supply hot water to the gently hissing radiators around the auditorium. The Royal Albert Hall boasts what was, at the time, one of the world's largest organs and steam was generated to serve two engines that operated the bellows. One early account stated that the instrument had 10,000 pipes, 130 stops, 5 keyboards and a 10-octave range; playing it must have been like trying to sail a Dreadnought battleship single-handed. It was probably an inaccurate inventory, but the present organ is only slightly more modest.

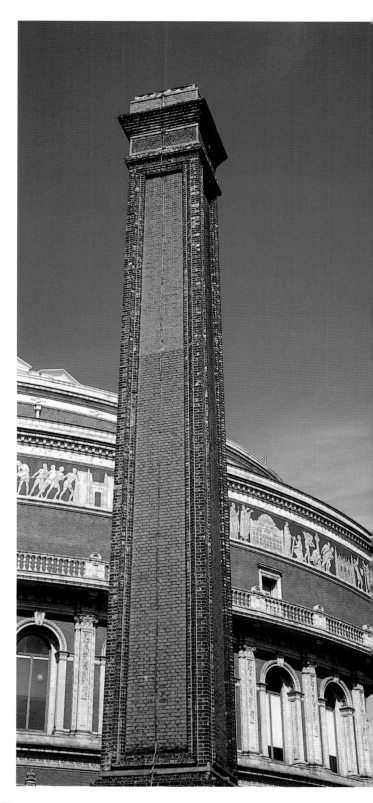

## Tower Bridge chimney ⊖ Tower Hill

There is so much to marvel at here on London's trademark bridge. A Gothic fairytale designed by Sir Horace Jones to chime with the Tower of London next door, this part suspension bridge, part lift bridge uniquely captures the imagination of Londoners and tourists alike. But how many of us give even a first glance at this little cast-iron fixture on the western balustrade of the northern approach?

It looks very much like one of the lamp standards without the light, but it is in fact a chimney that once served a fireplace far below that warmed a guardroom used by officials from the Tower. The ironfounder's name and address is still perfectly visible on the flue: Durham Brothers, 205 Bow Road E.

## Rotherhithe Road Tunnel ventilators ⊖ Shadwell or Rotherhithe

The Rotherhithe Road Tunnel was built in 1904–8. Costing half a million pounds it was the second road tunnel under the Thames after Blackwall and was once a very useful short cut for me on my way home to Kent if I suddenly was taken with the idea of visiting The Grapes in Limehouse.

Although now vital for the release of car fumes and the circulation of air, tunnel ventilators were originally built on such a large scale to allow for the escape of the miasma emanating from horse manure deposited on the carriageway below. The two ventilators for Rotherhithe are classical red brick rotundas that look like roofless Edwardian bandstands, particularly appropriate as the one on the north shore of the Thames (*left*) sits in the King Edward VII Memorial Park in Shadwell. This one is the most visible, the south shore ventilator being stuck in a yard with security gates.

## Circle Line ventilators, Cornhill & King William Street ⊖ Bank

James Greathead (1844–96) invented the travelling shield that facilitated so much of the tunnelling for London's underground railway system. His statue (*right*) shows him in broad-brimmed hat, casually looking at a plan with his overcoat over his arm. It was erected here in 1994, sculpted by James Butler RA. But look carefully under the figure and you will see an elliptical mesh that gives away the fact that the monument doubles up as a ventilator for the Circle Line underneath. The building in the background is the Royal Exchange.

Another ventilator around the corner in King William Street (*below*) is disguised as a classical pillar with suitable decorations. For all the world looking like some lost remnant of a forgotten age, the news vendor who shares the space next to the entrance to Bank Station reliably informs me that it's only about 10 years old.

For all their perceived starchiness the Victorians certainly had fun with their buildings. The craze for past styles found manifestations in just about every building type: churches (of course), schools, houses, railway stations, water works. Civic pride came very high on the list, so municipal buildings got more than their fair share of polychrome brick and terracotta. So something that was both municipal and to do with water got double points even before pen was put to paper.

### Wanstead Pumping Station ⊖ Redbridge

This 1901–3 Tudor-style pumping station (*top left*), by engineer W B Bryan of the East London Waterworks, is very difficult to see. The only view (unless one is a guest of Thames Water) is through gaps between the houses in Royston Gardens, just off the Redbridge roundabout. The impressive red brick tower is crowned with ball finials on the parapet and closes itself off to prying eyes with a huge door that would be more at home on a Victorian prison (*bottom left*). Tower and pumping station are in landscaped grounds next to the River Roding, together with a neat Waterworks Cottage by the entrance.

### Water tower, Lewisham ⇌ Ladywell

The 1884 water tower for the old swimming baths in Ladywell Road (*right*) is a structure that ticks off everything in the style book: red brick with blue brick outlining, cream terracotta arches and machicolation, and a fairytale oriel window with a tall slate roof. Even Pevsner called it 'jolly'.

## Abbey Mills Pumping Station, Abbey Lane
🚇 West Ham

When it came to sewage pumping stations the Victorians built veritable cathedrals, usually set in formal gardens of green lawns and shrubberies as if to distance themselves from some of the more doubtful aspects of their purpose. Sir Joseph Bazalgette recognised this and made sure that the works constructed to deal with the effluent flowing from his new London sewers were magnificent and hygienic manifestations of high Victorian ideals – cleanliness next to godliness and all that.

Abbey Mills (1868) is the best of four stations brought on stream to do the business, as it were, of pumping sewage up into the Northern Outfall Sewer that carried everything off to the treatment works at Beckton Reach. This sewer is like a railway embankment running along the eastern edge, now a 'Greenway' path from which the best, perhaps only, good views of the exterior can be had without scaling perimeter fences. The style is what they call 'Venetian Gothic', but with rows

of Byzantine windows and a stunning central lantern that wouldn't look out of place on the Kremlin. The whole effect was completed with two tall chimneys crowned with minaret cowls, but these were demolished in the Second World War to avoid their use as markers by the Luftwaffe, leaving their bases looking like churchyard mausoleums. Inside the effluent was pumped by eight Cornish beam engines; these were superseded by electric equivalents but the pumps still worked away in a temple of wrought-iron staircases and decorative cast-iron columns.

## Pickering Place, St James's ⊖ Green Park

It's very easy to walk past Pickering Place without noticing it's there. I only spotted it because a chap came out of it into St James's Street like someone striding out of a brick wall in a Harry Potter film. It is very narrow, opening out into a tiny square with a little sundial in the middle. But that's not the Peculiar. Going back down the alley I noticed the walls were lined with glossily painted wooden panels. Closer inspection revealed that some of them had dissected parts of lettering on them in signwriters' gilt done in the same style and legend that graces the frontage of Berry Bros & Rudd next door at No. 3 St James's Street. I assumed that they were doors to some additional storage space.

Berry Bros can trace their history back to 1698, making them indisputably one of the oldest wine merchants in the world. Their cellars spread out underground as far as Pall Mall, at 8,000 square feet the largest working cellars in London. That's space for 10,000 bottles. But this is no off-licence; you don't come in here and ask for a bottle of Blue Nun, as evidenced by the sloping wooden floors, oak-panelled walls and a curious sit-on weighing machine that has endured the likes of both Lord Byron and Evelyn Waugh.

On the pretext of checking out the case rate on some obscure Burgundy, I asked about the wooden-lined alley next door. The reply: 'They are our window shutters, sir.' They don't put them up every night, only at weekends. What a wonderful thing – heavy boards coated in countless coats of dark green paint, slid in order into grooves running down the alley.

## Borough Market, Southwark
## ⊖ London Bridge

Ever since Londoners have needed a market
there's been one here in Southwark, more or
less on this same site where roads from the
south and east converged at the river. In
1756 this site grew to be what is now the
oldest wholesale fruit and vegetable market in
central London, one that can boast of records
that go back to 1014.

A walk around Borough Market is one of
the best things you can do in London. Come
here at 2am and you'll see the lorries arriving
with fresh fruit and vegetables and the
'pitching porters' unloading them. By 9am it's
all over. Come here at the weekends and get
stuck into the gourmet market. Come here at
any time and just wander about amongst the
discarded cabbage leaves and empty barrows
with their artificial grass covers. As you look
up at the Schedule of Rents and the newly
regilded quatrefoil motifs on the roof spans,

listen out for trains lumbering overhead as
they make their way across it all from London
Bridge Station to Cannon Street. Better still
get on a train that does just that so that you
can get a Dickensian impression of the backs
of houses and the almost Cotswold-like
Southwark Cathedral. And remember to take
a look around the surrounding streets, all
showing the influence of the market.

On a corner in Park Street is this doorway
(*right*), whispering its past existence as if
trying to maintain some faint Gallic presence in
a street that also has a wonderful dairy that
extols the quality of a huge variety of English
cheeses. Best of all though is the stencilled
admonishment to the right of the door,
typically rendered inarticulate by someone
else's addition. This is the kind of thing I love
about London, that someone should go to this
much trouble to metaphorically poke you in
the ribs – a streetwise version of Magritte's
painting of a pipe perversely titled 'Ceci n'est
pas une pipe'.

## Tobacco Indians, St James's Street
⊖ Green Park

These two wooden Native American Indians stand on the pavement outside cigar merchants James J Fox and Robert Lewis in Mayfair. As rare as the sight of someone in the street chuffing away on a big Cuban cigar, they are a reminder of an age when tobacco was not being roundly condemned by the new puritans. Considering that the Native Americans were disenfranchised of their lands so that the colonists could grow tobacco, it may seem slightly odd that their image has been used so widely in the promotion of the product, but they are nevertheless as much a part of American iconography as clapboard churches and pumpkin patches. Probably more at home on a sidewalk in Council Bluffs, Iowa, they are a very welcome addition to the London streetscape, still advertising cigar stores whose names must by now have vanished in a ring of blue smoke from a five-cent Old Honesty cigar.

The atmosphere of the shop behind the figures is like an exclusive gentlemen's club, a world of humidors, leather armchairs and green-shaded lamps. Cigars can be bought by the case like fine wine, your favourite Bolivar or Partagas lovingly labelled and stored for you until required. Naturally Winston Churchill was a regular customer, even having his own chair to relax in whilst they sorted out his supplies of Romeo y Julieta and La Aroma de Cuba cigars.

## Michelin Building, Fulham Road
## ⊖ South Kensington

The wonderfully ebullient exterior of the Michelin Building hid a functionality that was perfectly in sync with the burgeoning motor age. Opened in 1911 this was the UK headquarters for Michelin, the French company from Clermont-Ferrand that led the world with pneumatic tyres. The front entrance, where you can now buy lobsters

and flowers from suitably Gallic Citroën *camionettes*, was the tyre-fitting bay and, as your car was put on to a six-ton weighbridge, you could wait for new tyres by passing the time in the Touring Office consulting maps and guides.

The designer of this *tour de force* in Brompton Cross was François Espinasse. We know virtually nothing about him, other than he worked for Michelin; the only other building he appears to have designed was the

company's more subdued head office in Paris. He made the entire London building a brightly coloured three-dimensional advertisement, his starting point obviously the cigar-chomping Bibendum, the Michelin man made from tyres. Much of this was achieved by the use of 'Marmo' facing tiles, something of an experiment for the manufacturers, Burmantofts. But perhaps some of the most heart-stopping moments come with the 34 tiled panels that race down Sloane Avenue and Lucan Place. Here the successes of Michelin tyres in cycle and motor races are celebrated in ceramic tiles designed by Ernest Montaut and manufactured by Gilardoni Fils et Cie. They continue around the entrance hall inside. For the superb restoration of this remarkable building we must be grateful for the collaboration in the mid-1980s of Paul Hamlyn and Terence Conran, whose offices and emporium now occupy the site.

## Wippell's, Tufton Street
⊖ St James's Park, Westminster

Wippell's were originally 18th-century Devon grocers, but now provide a kind of one-stop shop for men of the cloth. Here you can get kitted out with dog collars and amazing technicoloured shirts, enrobe a complete choir in cassocks and surplices, and then put in an order for some stained glass. Wippell's head office is still in Exeter, but they also have a weatherboarded branch in the USA and this shop in Tufton Street. Conveniently in the environs of Westminster Abbey ('Pop round to Wippell's and get me a new mitre, would you?'), this is another perfect example of London's specialist shops for the cognoscenti.

The carved wooden frontage is an extraordinary sight and something of a mystery until I got talking to Wippell's. Apparently these premises were originally occupied by Gawthorp's, who were monumental stonemasons. It looks like a half-hearted attempt had been made many years ago to remove their name from underneath Wippell's (*bottom left*), less successfully on their hanging sign – presumably they stayed on to take orders for gravestones. But their Romanesque figure (*right*) is still there, holding tools of the stonemason's trade in his right hand and what looks like a highly decorated capital in the other.

## Alexandra Palace
### ⇌ Alexandra Palace
### ⊖ Wood Green

Ally Pally. Just the nickname shows the affection and esteem that is held for this vast hilltop exhibition and events building. And quite right too. This is the north London equivalent of the Crystal Palace, which was moved to the heights of Sydenham after the Great Exhibition of 1851 and spectacularly burnt down in 1936. What is it about fire and these enormous palaces for the people? Alexandra Palace was opened in 1873; 16 days later it was a smouldering ruin. Rebuilt immediately, another conflagration in 1980 saw giant flames once again searing through the building.

But it's still here, indomitable but slightly odd and awkward on its hill with just about the best views possible of the rest of the capital. The designers were engineer Sir Charles Fox and Owen Jones (who had been extensively involved in the Crystal Palace). Their original project foundered, but by the 1860s the huge Italianate arches and glass domes were shaping up and a railway reached the Palace in the same year as the 1873 opening, trains running into a terminus (now closed) on the north side of the building.

## Alexandra Palace continued

So what did intrepid Victorian Londoners get
up to at Ally Pally? The Alexandra Palace Daily
Programme (price one penny) for the August
Bank Holiday of 1881 reads like an extended
version of the Beatles' song *Being for the
Benefit of Mr Kite!*: Dr Holden, Little Salvini,
'Trial by Jury', Clown Cricketers, Circus,
Drums and Fifes, Giant Punch and Judy,
Shadow Pantomime and the Destruction of
the Spanish Armada, along with much else
besides.

Alexandra Palace is also linked with the
early and, as it happens, more recent days of
the BBC. On the south-east corner tower is
an incongruous mast, 220 feet high (*above*).
A reminder – as it says on a Blue Plaque up
on the wall – that 'The World's First Regular
High Definition Television Service was
inaugurated here by the BBC 2nd November
1936'. At first it was two hours worth of
television but only within a radius of 25 miles.
The receivers – flickering 10-inch blue screens
mostly showing people playing music – were
almost prohibitively expensive, And then it all
came full circle when the mast was featured
in 'The Idiot's Lantern', a 2006 *Doctor Who*
episode where 1953 Coronation viewers were
brainwashed by Maureen Lipman.

## Turkish baths, Bishopsgate Churchyard
⊖ Liverpool Street

Sometimes the seemingly unstoppable tide of development just has to back off and leave things as they are. This little building just off Bishopsgate Churchyard is still here only because somebody very firmly said 'No'. Originally built as a Turkish Baths by Harold Elphick this was the mystical East arriving in an exotic rush of polychrome tiles and glass at the end of the 19th century. Even after it survived the Blitz they wanted to sweep it away in the mad excesses of the 1980s, but by now this was the Gallipoli Restaurant owned, very appropriately, by a Turkish gentleman. We must be very grateful to Mr Mourat for seeing off the predations of developers and demolition men, ensuring the survival of this exquisite little architectural gem. Allegedly based on the 19th-century shrine at Jerusalem's Church of the Holy Sepulchre, it is a remarkable survivor that has seen many different names emblazoned on the walls since those first steamy days in 1895.

## Palaces of Arts and Industry, Wembley
## ⊖ Wembley Park

*How well I remember the Palace of Arts,*
*massive and simple outside, almost pagan in*
*its sombre strength...*
　　John Betjeman, *Metroland* film commentary, 1973

In 1924 the British Empire Exhibition spread
over 216 acres in Wembley. Here the far-flung
colonial outposts gathered together in the
mother country: New Zealand showing off
dairy farms, Australia demonstrating how
much cotton it grew, India waving the flag
with elephants and pictures of the Taj Mahal
and Canada amazing the world with a model
of the Prince of Wales made out of butter.
The whole shebang was opened by King
George V on radio and then both king and
queen sat bolt upright on a miniature railway
as it hurtled amongst the pavilions and
amusements.

　　There were the usual exhibition
novelties like a kiosk made up of a
ziggurat of Sharp's Toffee tins
topped out with a parrot and one
with a giant globe crowned with
an Oxo cube. But the biggest
impact came with the purpose-built

pavilions – Palaces of Industry, Arts and
Engineering – and towering over them all the
Empire Stadium, opened the year before to
accommodate the 1923 FA Cup final. They
were to 'evoke the permanence of the
imperial glories of antiquity' and the palaces
with their windowless reinforced concrete
walls certainly had a whiff of the Egyptian
tomb about them.

　　The twin-towered stadium, beloved by
generations of shouting football fans, has
gone, replaced by a gargantuan manifestation
of truly awesome budgets that will allow
90,000 people to watch footballers being sent
off. Almost everything else except Wembley
Park Station has also vanished, but out in the
muddy nexus of the new stadium are two
silent, battered survivors. Along Engineers
Way – the Exhibition's 'Fairway of the 5
Nations' – are the Palace of Industry and the
much smaller Palace of Arts. Now just
warehouses (they once kept BBC television
scenery here) they nevertheless give a brief
flavour of how it once was. Look closer and
you will see part of the Exhibition's emblem
that graced posters, programmes, tea
caddies and tins of Jacob's Biscuits:
the superbly stylised British lion
designed by Frederic Herrick.

## LONDON RIVERSIDE

### Eel Pie Island, Twickenham ⇌ Twickenham

*Places like this produced the kind of person that sailed the little boats across to Dunkirk and we'd better not forget it.*

Ian Nairn, *Nairn's London*, 1988

Twickenham waterfront suffered wartime damage, but the usual execrable development proposals for it came to nothing. So you can still sit by the Thames under the trees and contemplate a walk down to The White Swan and Marble Hill House or just the view across to Eel Pie Island. This is one of London's little communities that would like to pull up a drawbridge and remain intensely private, but sadly it is no longer all weatherboarded shacks painted marine colours and housing eccentrics. Since a disastrous fire some years ago, there appears to be a move towards the inclusion of homes that would be more at home in Romford.

Eel Pie Island was once called Twickenham Ait and up until 1957 could only be reached by boat. Now there's a footbridge (no cars here) curving over the river to a little wooded island that has about 50 homes and 120 people living in them. In 2005 writer Danny Wallace tried to claim the territory for himself and start a new country until he was disabused of the notion by the local council. There's still an air of being somewhere special, but I particularly like the make-do-and-mend atmosphere of the boatyards with rivercraft snuggling up to each other against the shore.

Some will remember the now-vanished Eel Pie Island Hotel as a 1960s rock and R&B venue, playing host to the likes of John Mayall's Bluebreakers with Eric Clapton, The Yardbirds, Pink Floyd and the Rolling Stones. The Eel Pie Studios were here, owned by The Who's Pete Townshend, who appropriated the name Eel Pie for his publishing interests.

## Experimental lighthouse, Trinity Buoy Wharf
### DLR East India

This is the only lighthouse in London. It needs perseverance to find it, out on the Leamouth Peninsular in Orchard Place where the River Lea does one final meander by Canning Town before reaching the Thames. A marvellously airy spot, the wharf looks out across to the Dome and apart from interesting nauticalia in every corner – including this spruce red lightship (*left*) – it is also home to Fatboy's Diner and Container City (see pp 90–1 and 92–3).

Trinity House looks after our navigational warning devices and this was where they experimented with different forms of lighthouse illumination. The lighthouse itself was designed by Sir James Douglass in 1866 and it's here that they would have lit up the Thames with their trials of 'Argand', 'Matthews Incandescent' and 'Hood Petroleum Vapour' burners. Michael Faraday once laboured away on lenses in the workshop next door. In the first half of the 20th century, lighthouse keepers were trained here before being sent out to cliff tops and isolated offshore rocks. Is this where they also learned how to make those special tucks and creases in sheets so that they fitted the beds in odd-shaped lighthouse rooms?

Up in the lighthouse there's something even odder going on now. Jem Finer and Artangel have installed 'Long Player', 20 minutes of sound made by Tibetan 'singing bowls', continually repeated but computer-generated so that the exact same sequence will not be repeated for a thousand years. But how will we know?

## Fatboy's Diner, Trinity Buoy Wharf
**DLR East India**

Sometimes there are some wonderfully incongruous arrivals in London. Here is a sight one would normally expect to see in the Midwest, a genuine American diner with as much chrome and red leather as you can eat, chocked up on a quayside on the Leamouth Peninsular. Built in Elizabeth, New Jersey, in 1941 it was soon shipped out to River Road in Harrisburg, Pennsylvania. It rested on the banks of the Susquehanna for 49 years before going to Maine to be restored in 1990, eventually arriving here on this quayside in 2002. Apart from the very idea of it – and the fabulous coffee and fries – one thing pleases me over everything else. It gets the best seal of approval possible, a mention in the newly revised *London 5: East* volume in the *Buildings of England* series.

Even if one hasn't travelled on US highways, this streamlined silver prefab with its Pepsi bottle-cap roof badge is as much a part of our American dream as Greyhound buses and Simon and Garfunkel records. Apart from the obligatory yellow and red plastic sauce bottles, every table has chrome napkin dispensers and jukebox selectors that look like 1950s toasters. And every minute that goes by you expect, at the very least, that an orange-sunglassed Rod Steiger will turn up in a blue and white Plymouth.

## Container City, Trinity Buoy Wharf
**DLR** East India

Container City (*left and below left*) is just that, low-cost work places made out of corrugated steel shipping containers. To complete the maritime feel they have big portholes for windows and bright colour schemes that fit perfectly into the nautical style of the wharf with its red lightship and buoys. This is such a brilliant idea I wish I'd had it instead of the Urban Space Management people and Nicholas Lacey & Partners.

Although only 2mm thick, the steel is immensely strong and each container weighs in at 4 tons. But when stacked like children's bricks they remain completely rigid, even at five storeys high. Where have they been and what's been in them? Just about everywhere I should think and filled with everything but the kitchen sink, which, of course, is now in there somewhere.

## Greenwich Millennium Village
⊖ North Greenwich

On the other side of the river from Container City only slightly more conventional housing can be found on what is now known in estate-agent speak as the Greenwich Peninsular. This was Bugsby's Marshes and all you could once see in most directions was the largest gasworks in Europe. On 300 acres of hopefully decontaminated soil, Ralph Erskine & Partners have designed apartment blocks that group together like a wild afternoon with the Lego. Plotted out with coloured squares and rectangles, this high-rise village is the perfect foil to its near neighbour with its legs in the air, the impossible to please but nevertheless utterly brilliant spaceship called the Dome.

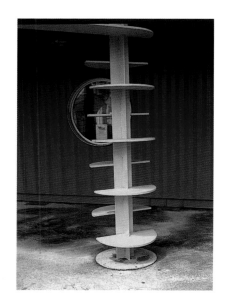

## Wapping Old Stairs ⊖ Wapping

Forty years ago one could still come out of Wapping Underground station at night and be regaled by the pungent scents of spices and tobacco drifting around the cobbled streets. The two or three other passengers that had alighted from the train with you would seemingly be immediately absorbed into the fabric of the tall riverside warehouses, so urgent was their desire to be about their business. One really had only one decision to make: turn right for the Prospect of Whitby or left for The Town of Ramsgate. Pubs, of course.

The latter is so named because apparently it was here that fishermen from Ramsgate landed their catches at Wapping Old Stairs, at the end of a narrow alleyway at the side of the pub (*top left*). Beware going down here at night at high tide; your only warning of the river may be the sound of water violently slapping against the stones. Descending down from the gloom of the alley you find a comparatively new set of steps, but from the backyard of the pub some original stairs can be seen (*right*).

Of course, a place like this literally drips with stories. Captain Bligh and Fletcher Christian drank in the pub before embarking on their world cruise on the *Bounty* and press-ganged naval crews were kept manacled down in the cellars. Any number of pirates were lead up the stairs prior to being hanged on Execution Dock, the site of which is now overlooked by the Captain Kidd pub, named after one of the more famous privateers. Some were simply tied in chains to a post to await drowning from the rising tide, their corpses only removed after three high waters. Could this be a remnant of that practice (*bottom left*), still being battered by the eternal surge of the tide?

## Woolwich Ferry ⇌ North Woolwich

Ferries are the oldest form of river crossing and we know that there was one here in Woolwich in 1308 because there's a record of someone paying a tenner for it. The present ferry was conceived in the 19th century by the Metropolitan Board of Works and, although they planned and constructed it, London County Council took the Board over two days before the opening in March 1889 and appropriated all the credit for it. Steam-powered boats – seen here in archive

photographs – were used up to 1963. The evocative picture of the *John Benn* coming into service in 1930 (*below left*) was taken from the decks of a Thames vessel. This ferry boat was named after a one-time member of London County Council, Sir John Benn.

Unless we are regular users we tend to forget that a vehicle ferry still plies across Gallions Reach between Woolwich and North Woolwich. We may hear on a radio traffic report that it's running OK, and indeed it does; the ferry runs seven days a week except on Christmas and New Year's Days. The only thing likely to stop services is if the captain can't see either shore because of fog; if this happens and you're on foot you can use a white-tiled tunnel that opened in 1912. The Woolwich Free Ferry has three vessels in use – the *Ernest Bevin* (whose aerial bridge can be seen here, *opposite*), the *John Burns* and the *James Newman* – and the whole enterprise takes only 15 minutes: 5 to load, 5 to cross and 5 to unload.

It is the riverine meeting place of the North and South Circular Roads (so much more romantic than their western union on Kew Bridge) and I did hear a rumour about a baby being born on it in the 1940s. My researches concluded that this wasn't Bryan Ferry.

## Body of work ⊖ Tower Hill

London just loves getting its kit off. Particularly, it may seem, around the Tower of London. Across the road in Trinity Square is the formidable ex-Port of London Authority building, designed by Sir Edwin Cooper in 1912–22. As if wanting to take on the Normans opposite it dominates the area with its own huge mausoleum of a tower. By the entrance are lamp standards (*left*) – with these iron boys cresting the waves of an iron sea – that fall in with the whole Edwardian idea of wanting to make a big impression.

Over the road is Edwin Lutyens' Mercantile Marine Memorial with its sunken garden extension, which was designed by Sir Edward Mauffe in 1955. Grouped in a semicircle around the garden are panels sculpted by

Sir Charles Wheeler, including this Puck-faced boy riding a dolphin by the simple expedient of putting a rope in its mouth, flanked by fishes and a row of seahorses in diminishing sizes like Russian dolls (*below left*). In *London Peculiars* (2004) I featured a beautifully languid mermaid, another Portland stone panel from this monument. This is a truly fabulous public display, which is usually overlooked by everybody fighting to get into the Tower or to hang over the bridge.

Just on the north-east side of Tower Bridge is an open space in front of an utterly brutal concrete monster of a hotel. As if to show just how good life could be by comparison, here is David Wynne's 1973 sculpture of a girl flying upside down in tandem with a dolphin, both spiralling round a jet of water rising up from a pool (*below right*).

## Fortune Theatre, Russell Street
⊖ Covent Garden

This classic Art Deco nude leans casually against a diamond-patterned frieze on the wall of the Fortune Theatre, high above Russell Street in Covent Garden. She gazes down steadfastly with great assurance, gently rubbing her right foot against her left leg. This compact theatre was designed by architect Ernest Schaufelberg and opened in 1924, the first London theatre to do so after the First World War. It shares a 'hanging freehold' with the Scottish National Church next door in which a corridor in the church dovetails with the auditorium and Dress and Upper Circles of the theatre. Schaufelberg was also the sculptor of the girl.

## Regent's Place, Euston Road
⊖ Euston Square, Warren Street

Two identical naked cast-iron men stare at each other, a sheet of plate glass dividing them. Who is the doppelgänger? And who is the *Reflection*, the title of Antony Gormley's 2001 sculpture that stands mutely in (and out) of the reception area at British Land's offices on Euston Road. Gormley is best known for the *Angel of the North* at Gateshead and *Another Place*, 100 iron men that temporarily stood in and out of the sea at Crosby in Lancashire before wading off to New York. Gormley's figures are always cast from his own body, which I suppose keeps the costs down a bit.

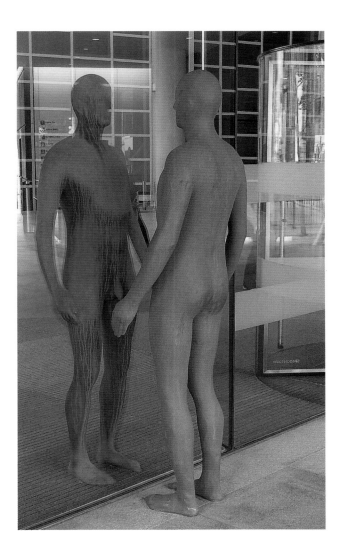

## Temporary girls
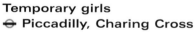 **Piccadilly, Charing Cross**

It's a little odd to give Underground station instructions for Peculiars that may have disappeared from the London streetscape when this is read, but, however impermanent, they nevertheless show how London still surprises us in the most startling ways. Here are two very temporary, very contemporary, pregnant girls out in the London summer sun.

Damien Hirst's *The Virgin Mother* strides across the forecourt of the Royal Academy on Piccadilly, aloof from the craned necks trying to work out just what exactly is going on. The pose is Edgar Degas's *Little Dancer*, but any resemblance ends there in a 35ft-high statue that consists of 13½ tons of metal. This statue is a reminder that the early days of teaching anatomy were sheer entertainment, science as art. From one angle this pregnant girl is wholly traditional, from another she is folded open to show us foetus, skull, muscles and tissue. All to the sound of fountains and gasps of astonishment in the courtyard.

Moving on to Trafalgar Square four plinths can be seen. One has never had anything on it, until someone had the brilliant idea of using it not for equestrian kings or Victorian generals, but for temporary displays of sculptures or ideas. So on this hot summer afternoon

sculptor Marc Quinn's pregnant white marble girl coolly ignores both the tourists thrashing about in the square's fountains and the pigeon on her thigh. The model is Alison Lapper, born without arms and shortened legs due to a chromosomal condition known as Phocomelia. Quinn said that he 'felt the square needed some femininity ... Alison's statue could represent a new model of female heroism.'

## Royal Waterloo Hospital, Lambeth ⊖ Waterloo

This 1905 former hospital, just opposite the Imax cinema in Waterloo, is said to be in the 'Lombardic Renaissance' style. The frontage has three tiers of *logge*, open arcades on each storey where patients could sit out in the sun. However, if there was any doubt about the building's function, then there are fascias of green Doultonware lettering telling us, amongst other things, that this is the Royal Waterloo Hospital for Children and Women. And if all that Art Nouveau lettering isn't enough, there is also a nude girl offering what looks like a stethoscope to the wind that blows her luxurious hair out across the sectioned panels. At their Lambeth works Doulton also created nursery panels for hospitals; the ones that originally decorated the Royal Waterloo were removed to St Thomas's Hospital.

## ARP stretcher railings, Harleyford Street
### ⊖ Oval

The ARP (Air Raid Precautions) first aiders were called stretcher parties in the London Blitz. On hand as soon as the 'all clear' had sounded from the rooftop sirens, they became the frontline in treating the injured after bombing raids on the capital. In *Wartime 1939–1945* Juliet Gardiner writes that they 'would arrive to treat minor injuries on the spot and gently lift the more seriously injured on to stretchers – or a door or plank if no stretchers were available – and into vehicles'.

Britain was generally ill-prepared for the Second World War, but plans for dealing with the aftermath of devastating air raids quickly saw stores filling up with metal stretchers and tens of thousands of papier mâché coffins. Surprisingly most of them were not required and the biggest problem was that large sections of the population were rendered homeless.

Inevitably the late 1940s saw a huge demand for housing in the grimy, battered, war-torn capital and planners became very excited at the possibilities for urban renewal. But amongst all the drawing up of elevations, quantity surveying and sifting through fixtures and fittings catalogues, I wonder who first turned an ARP stretcher on its side and

thought 'Hmm, this would make a good council flat railing.' Certainly there was a readily available supply, so brick piers were designed to take them. So preposterous was the idea of such a purposeful object being so imaginatively recycled that they quickly achieved urban-mythic status. When I first saw these prime examples in Harleyford Street, opposite the Oval cricket ground, I must admit I did have a slight moment of doubt. Until I noticed the four little kinks in the supporting tubes, a simple utilitarian device to keep the stretcher off the ground or the floor of an ambulance.

CHURCHMAN'S CIGARETTES

AIR RAID PRECAUTIONS BADGE

## Coronet, Notting Hill Gate ⊖ Notting Hill

Frequenters of Notting Hill will know this curious domed building (*opposite*) as a cinema, just about the only decent building in a parade of spectacular drabness. It was built in 1898 as a theatre, an outing into the suburbs for architect W G R Sprague who was usually found in the West End adding to his portfolio of playhouses that includes Wyndham's, the Albery and the New Ambassadors. In 1916 it succumbed to the world of cinema, but the theatre was relatively untouched as can still be seen inside and in the well-preserved theatrical swags under the rooftop balustrade and palm fronds in the spandrels. On a summer's afternoon there can be a trick of the light and the imagination easily turns it into a street corner in 1930s Jerusalem.

As a cinema – at least when we frequented it 10 years ago – it was unique in allowing you to take in your own beer and to smoke without hindrance. Nevertheless we had to avoid the manager if he was lurking in the foyer because he had the doubtful habit of telling you what a good film you were about to see and, if you weren't careful, how it ended. Up at the back of the circle there were lavatories from which, if you propped the door open, you could still see the film.

## Caretaker's lodge, Flaxman Terrace ⊖ Euston

Over in Euston is another curious dome or two. On the corner of Flaxman Terrace and Burton Street is the caretaker's lodge (*this page*) for St Pancras Borough housing, designed in 1907–8 by Joseph & Smithem. Like the flats themselves the building is fenced in with Art Nouveau railings and has an authoritative air about it as if it really wants to be a police station.

## Pagoda, Kew Gardens ⊖ Kew Gardens

Horace Walpole caught sight of this building being built from his Gothick extravaganza at Strawberry Hill. Appalled at its height he complained '…in a fortnight you will be able to see it from Yorkshire'. Kew's 10-storey octagonal Pagoda is indeed tall for its time, 163 feet high with each storey a foot less in overall width so that the tower tapers up over the trees. This is a superb example of chinoiserie, the mania for all things Chinese that gripped garden designers in the mid-18th century. Designed by William Chambers, who also placed a now vanished Turkish Mosque and Alhambra in close proximity, it was completed in 1762. Chambers was the architect of choice of Princess Augusta, the Dowager Princess of Wales and mother of George III, and the Pagoda was built as a surprise for her. Imagine trying to keep such a thing secret.

Originally there were iron dragons enamelled in coloured glass snorting around each roof line, each with a bell in its mouth, and gilding on the summit; imagine the experience of coming into this south-east corner of Kew Gardens on a breezy day, clouds scudding across the sky as a brilliant chiming sounded over the trees and the gilding flashed in the sunlight. The slate roofs and dragons were removed to pay off George IV's debts.

In the mid-19th century Decimus Burton offered to replace them when he was engaged in designing the Palm and Temperate Houses, the supersize greenhouses away to the north, but the cost was prohibitive. Maybe Kew could get the Ministry of Defence to cough up; during the Second World War bomb designers made holes in each of the 10 floors of the Pagoda through which they dropped their latest prototypes in order to test the aerodynamics.

## Lud Gate survivors ⊖ Temple, Blackfriars

*Gather up the fragments that remain, that nothing be lost.'*

St John 6: 12

One darkening winter's afternoon I stepped off Fleet Street into the yard of St Dunstan's church in order to get a closer look at the lettering on the magazine offices next door (*see p 33*). Curious about something in the gloom of an entrance to the church vestry I discovered these sepulchral figures (*top left*) backed up against the wall as if engaged in some macabre game of hide-and-seek.

Like so much in London, these curiosities have travelled the metropolis like lost souls, in this case since the 16th century when they originally adorned a new replacement for the Lud Gate, one of the entrances to the City. They are in fact depictions of King Lud and his sons and once stared down towards the Fleet River at what is now Ludgate Circus. This traffic calming measure was sold for £148 in 1760 and the Lud Gate was pulled down. The statues – including the one of Elizabeth I in her niche (*bottom right*) – were removed but rescued by the Marquis of Hertford who used them as garden ornaments at his Regent's Park villa. However, the next century saw them brought here when St Dunstan's was rebuilt in 1829–33. Every reference I have come across concerning King Lud, with or without his offspring, is very vague about his origins. Some think he gives his name to London itself; many agree that he could have been a king ruling around the time of the Roman invasion; others think he was just a made up kingly figure used for political purpose. Man or myth he will always be associated with London's more shadowy histories.

Some time later I nearly tripped over a stone (*bottom left*) embedded in a corner of Pilgrim Street, just off Ludgate, only to discover that this too was a survivor of the old gate. It may have been placed here to protect the building from vehicle wheels in the narrow confines of the lane.

### Dryden Street ⊖ Covent Garden

One is always rewarded for looking up. Covent Garden has many reminders of its fruit-and-vegetable market past, often expressed in high warehouse doors and iron hoists restored as design features for offices and loft apartments. Here in Dryden Street is something extra: moulded relief plaques showing a beautiful queen or princess in restful repose. Is there a connection here with Restoration Poet Laureate John Dryden, or is it a reference to the name of some long-forgotten market wholesaler – 'Princess Potatoes' perhaps? Or maybe she is just a stock item from the building merchant's catalogue – 'Ere, how about 'er, she'd look nice, bit of pink paint, look lovely she would.'

## Victoria Embankment lamp posts
## ⊖ Temple, Embankment

We are not best served by modern lamp post design. We know they can't all be gas lamps with green-glowing Veritas mantles and George Formby leaning on them, or decorated with gilded dolphins and painted roses either. But a look in a Victorian ironfounder's stock catalogue shows designs that would suit most London streetscapes and there must be something better than the often ill-thought-out options that can be completely alien to their environment. We've got a big problem with inappropriate street furniture, quite apart from there now being far too much of it.

Underneath the Victoria Embankment runs Sir Joseph Bazalgette's cavernous brick sewers. They were joined in 1870 by the Metropolitan District Railway (now the Underground's District and Circle Lines) and these extraordinary lamp posts by the new roadside (*left and top right*). On the riverside parapet are lamps with big black dolphins twisted around the columns (John Ruskin hated them) and the motif is continued on a smaller scale here with four smaller gilded fish bubbling out from the corners of the base. On the pavement side red roses open up in stages.

## Seven Dials ⊖ Covent Garden

The last remnant of this lamp post (*bottom right*) can be seen in Covent Garden, the decoration shearing off and the lantern no longer lighting the street but still displaying the heraldry of a long-forgotten council. This is the coat of arms of the old Borough of Holborn, cast into the maintenance access panel that could only be opened with a hefty key.

## Temple Bar, Paternoster Square ⊖ St Paul's

The Temple Bar was talked about at length in the first volume of *London Peculiars* and, as the book went to press, it returned to the City from the shrubberies of Theobald's Park in Hertfordshire. Originally this was a Restoration bottleneck between the Strand and Fleet Street, but it was taken down in 1878, eventually leaving town for brewer

Sir Henry Meux's country estate 10 years later. Now it hides round a corner from St Paul's Cathedral in Paternoster Square. Jonathan Glancey wrote in the *Guardian* '...it seems as out of place and as kitsch as a cheap, over-restored carriage clock on an overcrowded mantelshelf'. A little harsh, but I can think of at least 20 places it would have looked better. Its appearance will doubtless improve when London rains and

frosts have ravaged it somewhat, but at the
moment it has the slight air of an over-iced
wedding cake, an idea that perhaps could
be taken up by the cathedral shop next
door, which already flogs Temple Bar mugs
and candles. But at least the Portland stone
gateway is back in London where it belongs,
mended and scrubbed up with freshly
carved heraldic details and statues back in
the niches.

And so our wanderings around the capital draw to a close and we can put our feet up in a pub. The Seven Stars in Carey Street would be good, just around the corner from Lud & Sons and the Beano office. But before we do it's worth remembering that London Peculiars can come at us from all directions. Sometimes there's not an awful lot to say about them, but often they are really worth going out of the way for because there's always an interesting story, always something that marks them out from everyday London life.

Leon's is a fresh fast food restaurant on Ludgate Circus, but if you didn't know this and you're walking down Ludgate Hill all you see is this surreal hand offering you an orange out of the wall of a classical building. This is a beautiful image to come across on a hot day trudging the streets.

This blue door with Eleven and a Half written on it is in Spitalfields. The 'half' is presumably because Number Eleven has divided itself cell-like to provide another address in the same street, but the fact that it's written out rather than presented in numerals makes more of a point about it and adds a touch of humour.

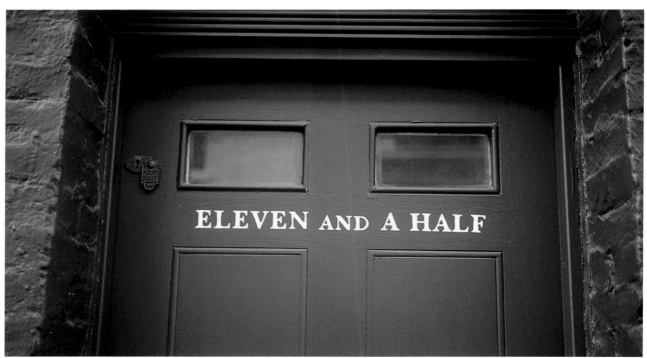

## Swiss Re Building, St Mary Axe
## ⊖ Aldgate, Liverpool Street

When a building like this appears in London, you know just about anything can happen. Dan Dare-style science fiction comes alive at 30 St Mary Axe. Everybody was so amazed and delighted when it first started to push its seductive shape up into the City skyline that the Swiss Re Building immediately got a nickname, always a good sign. The name Gherkin was first coined by a *Guardian* sub-editor, but the option I really like is Crystal Phallus. Much has been written about this breathtaking building but the basic facts are that it is 590 feet high, has 40 storeys and was designed by Foster & Partners. The most interesting fact, however, is that there isn't a curved piece of glass in it except at the very top where it's crowned with a lens-shaped cap.

It is also another example of how well-designed new buildings work in the streetscape of the City, happily, in my view, sitting alongside medieval churches and Victorian office blocks. This is because the City is still bound by the original medieval street pattern. Wren's post-Great Fire vision of baroque streets radiating out from the Monument was thwarted by opposition to the financial disruption that would have been caused if everything pre-Great Fire was swept away. So the restricted viewpoints still provide frames for the extraordinary, slow reveals for the unexpected.

I finish off this book with the Gherkin because it's proof that the very essence of London means that Peculiars are being created all the time and are not just fading ghosts still clinging on in backstreets and at the bottom of dark alleyways. And in any case this one just sticks out a bit more.

# FURTHER READING

Ashley, P 2004 London Peculiars. London: English Heritage

Ellmers, C and Werner, A 1988 London's Lost Riverscape. London: Viking

Gay, K 2005 Palace on the Hill. London: Hornsey Historical Society

Hessenberg, I (ed) 1986 London in Detail. London: John Murray

Jackson, P 1951 London is Stranger than Fiction. London: Associated Newspapers

Jackson, P and Snowden, W C 1953 London Explorer. London: Associated Newspapers

Jones, E and Woodward, C 1983 A Guide to the Architecture of London. London: Weidenfeld & Nicolson

Nairn, I 1988 Nairn's London (revisited by Peter Gasson). London and New York: Penguin

Pevsner, N et al various dates Buildings of England series (London volumes). Harmondsworth: Penguin and London: Yale University Press

Snowdon, A A and Headley, G 1999 London: Sight Unseen. London: Weidenfeld & Nicolson

Stamp, G 1984 The Changing Metropolis. Harmondsworth: Viking

Stevenson, G 2003 Palaces for the People. London: Batsford

Trench, R and Hillman, E 1984 London Under London. London: John Murray

# ACKNOWLEDGEMENTS

Sign on Shooter's Hill, SE18

These Peculiars come with particular thanks to, in alphabetical order:

Kathy Ashley, Bates of Jermyn Street, Lucy Bland, Simon Bland, Adèle Campbell, David Campbell, Simon Clarke, Ptolemy Dean, Rupert Farnsworth, Richard Gregory, Alan Hall at Wippell's, Gill and David Harris, Patricia Hastings, Leigh Hooper, Clémence Jacquinet, John Longbourne, Biff Raven-Hill, Joyce Raven-Hill, Rob Richardson, René Rodgers, Justin Savage, Margaret Shepherd, Iain Sinclair, Greg Southwell, Karen Southwell, David Stanhope, Urban Space Management, Philip Wilkinson, and the Worshipful Company of Goldsmiths.